Songs of Death
& OTHER VERSE

By

PEARL ANDELSON

FORGOTTEN POETS

Editor | Dick Whyte   Number 2 | 2022

PEARL ANDELSON (1899-1996) was born and raised on the West Side of Chicago. Andelson attended Chicago University where she joined the Poetry Club and met fellow poets Elizabeth Madox Roberts, Janet Lewis, Yvor Winters, and John Tiggo, among others. She began publishing in 1921, appearing in *Poetry*, *Voices*, *The Forge*, and *The Dial* – all popular outlets for the 'new verse' in English – and worked as a reviewer for Harriet Monroe's *Poetry* magazine. Andelson's first book of poems, *Fringe* (1923), was well received and verses continued to appear in journals throughout the 1920s. In a review of her work, Winters would write; "Andelson has developed and mastered a compact and beautiful technique that can apparently be made as simple or as intricate as she desires; and sometimes a cold bitter passion goes half-way to meet it... Here are precision, flawless juxtaposition, and an exquisite mastery of end and internal rhyme and of rhythm," having "those qualities of intensity and polish which are so admirable." Following this Andelson took a lengthy break from poetry, waiting over fifty years to publish her second collection, *Arch of a Circle* (1980), in collaboration with Doris Vidaver and Deborah Cohen.

Publication credits (an ellipses after the title indicates an excerpt): selected verses from *Fringe* (1923); some of which were first published in *Poetry* (1921-22), and Robert Morss Lovett (ed.), *Collected Verse by the Poetry Club of the University of Chicago* (1923); 'From A Bay Window' [epigraph], 'Solace' [in haiku form], & 'Song On Death' (*Poetry*, Dec. 1921); the second-half of 'A Trivial Day' [later cut], variants of 'Sea Girl' & 'Chapters' (Dec. 1922); '2 Poems' (*The Forge*, July 1924), '2 Poems' (Aug. 1924), & 'The Sleeper Awakened' (Spring 1925); 'A Swan' (Autumn 1926); 'And the Prophets' (*The Dial*, Oct. 1926); 'Identity', 'Abstract Moment', 'Motoring', 'The Lovers', 'My Mind', 'Boat Song', & 'Song' (*Poetry*, June 1926); 'Enlarged Dominion', 'Late Summer Day', 'The Lion', 'Alligator', 'Waiting', 'Sea-Walk', 'To A Child of Nine Months', 'Messiah', 'Dance', & 'Progression' (*Poetry*, Nov. 1928).

Cover: Marguerite Zorach – 'The Half Dome' & 'Yosemite Valley' (*The Dial*, Feb. 1921). Inside: 'Trees I', 'Trees II', & numerous ornaments (*Inland Printer*, June 1923, etc.); Mildred Heinau – 'Head', 'Schoolroom', & 'Flowers' (*The Dial*, Oct. 1926), etc.

FORGOTTEN PRESS
Aotearoa | New Zealand

ISBN: 978-1-991310-11-8 (paperback) ● 978-1-991310-12-5 (hardback)
978-1-991310-13-2 (ebook)

PEARL ANDELSON
SONGS OF DEATH & OTHER VERSE

FRINGES

A selection of verses from *Fringe*,
first published 1923.

OTHER POEMS

Assorted early, variant, and later verses,
published 1921-1928.

FORGOTTEN POETS
edited by **Dick Whyte**.

───── ❧ ❧ ─────

Missing Meters! Lost Lyrics! Vanished Verses!

FORGOTTENPOETS.COM

FRINGE

To My Father
and To Edna

With that surprise
Of one who speaks
To us and knows
Wherein he lies.

—Yvor Winters

Mishap

The rain arranged
crystal berries for me
to wear
in my hair.

By inadvertence one fell
into the
infinity
of a bluebell.

To a Bird in a Cage

O little yellow bird,
You are my soul,
Repeating a note
For which there is no word.

Expression

Inept as the words
That wait upon my mind
These twigs and half-formed buds,
Pecking the wind.

Worker in Marble

So I begin—
More bitter chiselled words.
Not one soft word
To ease my heart.

Solace

Tap
At my pane
With your finger-tip,
O rain.

Word

How soon
I, too,
Have been left lonely,
O pale moon.

Autumn Trees

Like old men
and women:
simplified
to a gesture.

Madonna

My eyes are infinitely mild:
Your hand,
Lying against my breast,
Is like a child.

Tide Out

But the hour comes,
When you are snuffed out
Like a ghost
At dawn.

At Play

My fingers
Are merry children
In the meadow
Of your hair.

From a Sea-girl

I

Star-light and moon-light
Slip into the doorways of the sea
All night.

II

My hair is the sun-color
Of the sand; but in an inland pool
My eyes were cool
As thin sea-air.

Woman in a Garden

Grey tulips; yellow tulips
Walk in wide
Companies beside
The woman in her garden.

She who walks thus apart,
Whose garden
Enters her heart,
Whose steps go—

Her eyes are dumb.
They know:
What miracle
Can come?

Thin Refuge

Are you more than
Man?

Go! I can
Say, *Go!* or I can

Take the veil of
Thought, fog-wall you
Cannot cleave through.

Spring Moon

One fair
Breast is bare.
Your eyes caress
This; mine the moon.

My lips a red
Flower; with a fine
Thread
Our souls are caught.

As ever your thought
Flees mine.

To Felix

Clear as water pooled in a cup
I hear your thoughts
Through all the spaciousness of my unrest.
You have no place
For the white bird at my breast,
Or the face your hands lift up.

April Snow

Oh, your words are bitter to me
As these last flakes of snow are
To the little shining buds; but no bud
That glistens like a raindrop on a tree
Is so fresh with love.

Seaside

Steam refrain to rain
of gravel. Long division
in the mind
running about with hods
carried over. Impossible to find
an answer true if found.

Panel

Slim birches make
A wall along the way
The women take, they

With remote air
Of eye and hand and
Coiled hair. Long-throated, they

That reach
Out down the birch-walk
In thought
Too still for speech.

I Take My Answer of a Sage

O black-gowned philosopher that walks
    on the water,
Precisely-cut as the evening star,
All mysteries are in your profound eyes
In one. Who tries to find you
Therefrom is drawn down.

Out of a Weariness

O Love,
Be Rest; be Calm.
(For I am wise!)
Come like Death
With quiet palm and eyes.

Philosophic Dialogue

1st Figure: Mountains are simple—
In the thumb-nail mind
Of man illusion doubles to
Illusion in semblance of
Complexity to hide
Confusion.

2nd Figure: None but knows
Within Six Days
He made the World
And on the Seventh
Sought Repose.

The Evil, dying,
Descend to Hell;
The Good come
Into the Kingdom.

1st Figure: Infinite Logic
Is too fine a
Web for the myopic
    eye of a
Fly.

2nd Figure:	None but knows Within Six Days—
1st Figure:	Cause follows cause without End. The hounds tear In a circle after a No-hare.
2nd Figure:	The Good come Into the Kingdom.
1st Figure:	For this is truth: the tail is Coiled back relevantly to the Teeth.
2nd Figure:	There is but This single beauty: In fear of God each Does his duty.
1st Figure:	Out of the logic of Compensation in a circle Autonomic, beauty to Spare, a girl's Breasts; her hair.
2nd Figure:	. . . fear . . . . duty.

Chapter

I

How long ago since I brought you
    into my heart
And you still stand,
Cold effigy of love,
Letting none pass.

II

Shadows
In a wind,
Two contend for place—
How shall I know my mind?

III

Like an unhappy ghost
I lingered
In the dark corners
Of his soul.

IV

His eyes
Are gray
And solitary
As the sea.

V

Do not drop your head,
So upon your breast—
My eyes hold all it was best
I leave unsaid.

In All

No bitterness remain,
If in all,
I have loved a passing shadow
Cast on a wall.

Portrait of an Old Lady

Up flutters a hand to caress—
Midway in the prayer—
Her Sabbath dress,
The frail gray of her hair.

Autumn Rain

To eyes hollow
With the gray distress
The passing swallow
Is all but a caress.

To an Erstwhile Loved One

Shall I, my friend,
Who knew satiety
In love and company,
Cry at this welcome end?

When I would breathe deep
Breaths, because my
Soul at last is mine,
Shall I weep?

Late Winter Wood

One cannot know
What words they whisper who go,

Unbeheld among the rooted deer
That herd here,

And without footsteps pass
Across the hard grass.

Two Sue for Favor

One is young.
Lonely his eyes.
The kiss of his lips
Salted with bitterness.

One is old and wise
With pale lips
And brittle
Finger-tips.

Excursion . . .

In the sand woods inland a spotted
    antelope stands,
and waits,
and fluctuates
among his spots.

The vertical waters flowing
horizontally with sky
and hills and into this my
going.

Sun
and moon one.

Out of an Early Snow

I see the forehead of Moses
In the autumn sky,
The prophet who could look
    into this dream
And prophesy.

He will not say.
Only rends
White wisps of hair
To go with the chipped tablet
Down the air.

A Miraculous Day in May

Before this,
One must have face,
Indeed, to offer a flower
In a vase.

The Philosopher

For hermitage: a grain
Of rice.
"Where assemble one's selves again
In all thy rooms?"

Sits in the sun, assumes
No airs.
"If ye be too precise
For bare shins, look not."

Sits in the sun.
"One
The beginning, and One
The end. Both the One?"

Willows bend in the wind.
So pliant to the next thought.
"God is good. One may see far,
Demanding nought."

Sehnsucht

In hooded procession
Night enters here,

Recession
Of light, not of love,

Not of the need of rest,
Transcending lip and breast,

Goad
That in Them created God.

Steeples

They gaily pass
Within
Who would be freed
    (*en masse*)
Of sin.

Connexion

A phasma hare
scampers in the chambers where,
feigning not to see,
I comb my hair becomingly.

Half-nun

Oh, believe me, I would rejoice,
If you could tell yourself:
"As well
Caress snow."

To a Dead Love

Why, O love,
Shall I cease to sing,
Who above her child
Would plant a flowering thing?

Legerdemain

While the cricket vaunted
Our rain-brilliant eyes,
A subtle thicket caught at
Half-lies.

A Trivial Day in Early Autumn

A China lily cup
Upon a pool
Lifts up
Its bowl.

Over the pale sky
Frail clouds;
A butterfly
About the garden flowers.

Autumn Evenings

Cleaving autumn from evening
white north-south walk,
imaginary line where we walk.

On a park bench I
quench I in gray air,
while memories of autumn trees
cry:
"Bring spring!"

Or savagely on the one sky
die.
But the moon is an eternal
pearl.

Or lake and sky a one
and I go
a curtain before the moon
on.

Other Poems

Holy
As God's word
Bird-
Notes heard.

From a Bay-Window

I

My world is a pane of glass.
These only
Of the shadowy without are mine:
They that pass;
The gray birds fluttering by;
The cloud that sometimes sails
Over the chimney-bitten sky,
When all else fails.

II

Knock at my pane
With your finger-tips,
O rain.

III

Subtle
The wind
Among
The fallen leaves.

IV

The grass
Is wanly brittle
Beneath the feet
Of those who pass.

Song on Death

Death comes inexorably. His pale deft hand
Is never still. Swift and impalpable
He comes, taking what he will. Life is a circle
Which has gone its round. He tarries
Where old women sit, peering at the ground.

Poems

I

We shall meet beyond body's rim,
Meet and mingle;
We dead neither out nor in,
Not merged, not single.

The little laughing word quite past,
A dull communal kiss;
My dear, we turn away too fast
From this.

The auburn-backness of your hair
Will be air;
Your distinct eyes,
Where?

II

I wore a hat and shoes and dress;
I wore a lucid smile,
The feet of my soul did scarcely press
Ground while.

And I was far and I was here
And God was near.
And God flowed like a sea
Through me.

He settled in the single islands
of my eyes;
Men viewed this with surprise.

III

With wonder filled
Stand I
Before a butterfly

Under a carved sky.
Do You
Worship a word?

Not I.
Brown, dotted,
    smaller than a bird
One with my heart
Heart one with all
All one, the same
We have no name.

IV

    Redder than cherry wine,
Minutely veined,
The petal of a peony in the hollow of a palm,
Both mysteriously grained.

The hand which is so thin and calm,
For all its mind is no more fine and strange,
    No more,
Than this it is hollowed for.

The Sleeper Awakened

In my far resting place I heard
Your word.
To this and to your kiss
I stirred.

When I think of that deep
Sweet slumber without breath,
A flower on my breast,
Marble in sleep;

No dream to torture
Lip and sight,
No alteration in my sleeping soul
Of day and night,
I could weep, I could weep.

And the Prophets in their Season

Autumn is the time to be unearthly wise.
All prophets mirror October skies.
The bush burns in autumn.
    Were my eyes
One shade more mad I should make
As clearly as did Moses and did Blake
The outline
Of God's figure shine
In burning bush and brake.

SLOW SONGS

Identity

My grandmother bore me
In my mother's womb.
What there is more of me
My lovers assume.

Winter and summer modify
The whole.
How ever shall God descry
My soul?

Abstract Moment

I who so quietly walked
The streets of thought,
Intently dividing entity
By eternity,
Had neither eyes nor lips; my hair
Was vague; and my breasts were spare.

Alone I walked.
My body was one with my thought.
The pulsing river and the bridge,
The architecture at their edge,
I could not find
Substantiated in my mind.

Motoring

The ripe red hills with trees thereon
Sat in the sun.
We passed in autos; our flight swallowed
The little houses in the hollows.
The sky flowed like a river
Over all forever.

The Lovers

They sped with love
Along its fruit-hung ways,
Neither knowing the face
Of the other, or whereof
He wove his days.

How shall they know or seek
Each the soul of each
Who taste of love as of a peach?

My Mind

On one day my mind, becalmed,
Shall lie in God's palm—
A seed so clear, so still,
A thousand winds,
A thousand bees,
Shall stir it not from Ease
    To Will.

Boat Song

The stars forever
Swim the river
Ferry me over!

We who move thither,
Wind in our hair,
Are here forever.

Song

The sky is yellow.
Our eyes are hollow.
I walk alone
On the beach stone.

My hand
Closed in your palm,
I walk alone and
I am calm.

The sallow sea
For company,
I walk alone
On the beach stone.

A Swan

Float, float on your shadow.
 Float over the lagoon,
Opal bird. The unreal pallor of the moon
Lurks in your curves. The opal
Of the moon adds oval to oval
Shadow above and under the lagoon.

Float, float on your shadow,
 white mist arisen.
Float in and out of my eyes. Glisten
Among the dust-green willow, still, remote.
Let me learn the bend of your throat
In an unending lesson.

Enlarged Dominion

There was an earth for me once more clear
Than this, when I walked in my own mind.
How near
All things were! Scarcely had I entity
    apart from them.
Myself was the robin in the yard,
    the new-flushed tulip on its stem.

My earth was smaller then by an earth or two—
And by as much more true.
Every bud, every bird, in the park of my mind
I knew; every beast, every rock.
I could foretell the turn of the wind.

    The stony certainties are gone.
All is confusion now, all diffuse. Will ever
    I put this new
World in order, the new sights and sounds
    that strew
Consciousness untidily every which way?
Perhaps I shall awake quite unprepared
    some day,
And from my open window see, hewn sure,
The new world orderly as the old, distinct
    and secure.

Late-Summer Day

The breath of autumn is on my hand.
I walk alone.
My hand is like the cool sand
And the cool stone.

A dull duck drags a bright trail.
Somewhere in the pale
Air or on the ground
A cricket sews a light seam of sound.

The breath of autumn is on my hand.
My eyes embroider a band
Of the crimson-bodied flies that pass
Deftly between blades of grass.

The Lion

The lion enters my heart; he lies at rest,
Most solitary beast, in a solitary breast.
He walks in the air of my most frail thought:
He crushes not a flower under foot.
We walk in his jungle, hand on mane;
On the sand-brown of his mane, how blue
    my every vein!
His jaw is kindlier than that of a mother:
Kind for me, kind for any other.

Alligator

Inert on his log,
Sea or ditch,
He sleeps like the dead
What matter which?

He breathes without breath.
A log to lie on,
The same are to him
Moment and eon.

Waiting

So must the root, ripening to stalk,
The push of spring, the pulse of April
     beat: the earth
Must wonder as I wonder, who walk
Wondering at the inner mystery,
     the imminent birth.

The doubting ground must question as I do:
Can the new, the unknown shoots show
     the usual bright green?
Can this year's unskilled flowers,
     pushing through,
Be perfect of petal as ever they have been?

No more than the hard brown ground can I
Foresee the mystery. Pulse of child in me
Or pulse of April in the earth, myself
     and the earth must lie
Our winter-span out before
     the living spring can be.

Sea-Walk

The women of the sea on pale mares
Gallop over, gallop under, the crystal water.
From the asphalt of the sea-walk unawares
I gather fragments of their laughter.

Daughters of the water, two and two and a third,
On chalk-white mares race and laugh, naught
But this in their minds. On the beach I go, naught
But this in my thought.

To a Child of Nine Months

Content to rest here where we are, my young son:
You an infant with soft sounds and soft ways;
Your eyes color of silver, bright as silver spun
Out of a mint into your little self. I like our days
Compact, and intimate, and closely knit.
I am content. This mine, I shall submit
To what you may or may not be.
My happiness demands no gift of prophecy.

Messiah

Complete, alive, belonging to itself,
    of her no part—
The girl looked down at this against
    her linen shift.
It beat against her heart. It beat: her Heart.
Her teat exposed, swollen with first milk,
    twitched.
The little creature wept. With finger and
    thumb upon the nipple pressed,
She offered her full breast.

Obedient to the first need, like a calf it
    sucked and found warm milk good.
Small red fists and bones delicate as a
    pigeon's bones. It's hair
Was like a flame upon a head or a crown.
    Whether of man begot or God
On the girl's heart it lay, contented there,
Taking its first slow milk without surprise.
After a while it turned and shut its eyes.

In the Dance

Grass-like to the wind
Of music, I a dancer.
My mind made answer
To your laughter.

You failed
To see, so vastly I contrived
    to please,
How far upon receding seas
My sight sailed.

Progression

Given a point on a circumference
Of life: this point is death, an inference
Of rest where no rest is possible, where
Atomic rush is ceaseless in still air.
Sun in the due course of change
Becomes moon, and possibilities range
Beyond the impossible. Death
Is but a swimmer's holding of the breath.
Life has no end. Man, with greatest and least,
Progresses to some outlandish god or beast,
In what unknown condition of sensory
    wealth or dearth,
To rule what polished planet unseen to earth.

> *This Space for Your*
> *Thoughts*

THE OLD EXPRESSIONS ARE WITH US ALWAYS
AND THERE ARE ALWAYS OTHERS

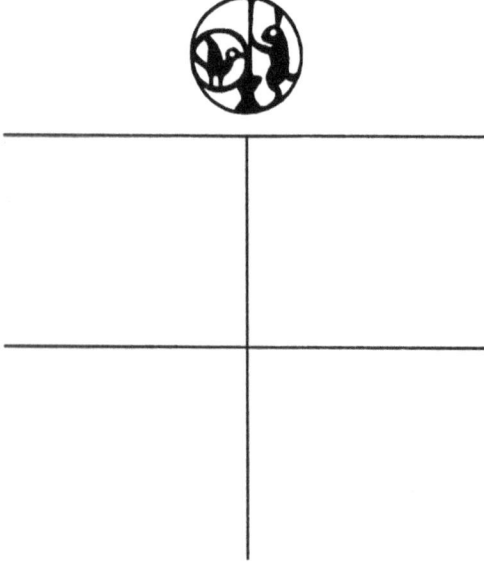

Please handle with care.